I HAVE LE

CW00742561

Jacqueline Woods

To Alexandra
with love
from,
Jacqueline
X.

PreeTa ✳ **Press**

Foreword

This is my second collection of poetry. I have decided to call
it 'I Have Learnt' in tribute to the poem by Jorge Luis Borges,
'You Learn' and my own version of that poem, 'I have Learnt'.
The poems in this collection explore the challenges and the
many joys I have experienced in getting older and becoming
a 'woman of a certain age.'

Some poems look back on childhood and some forward to
being older. The voluntary work I do with Age UK and The
Reader charity plus my own experiences have made me more
aware of the cruelty and complexities of dementia and disability.

I hope these poems will touch you and make you smile.

Jacqueline Woods

Dedication

To my wonderful children and grandchildren

Claire, Leslie, Alice
Rosa, Annabelle and Eva

"And you learn that you really can endure,
That you really are strong
And you really do have worth"
Jorge Luis Borger

Published in 2018 by
Preeta Press, Bolton,
Greater Manchester

preetapress.com

All Rights Reserved
Copyright Jacqueline Woods 2018

Illustrations by Julia Temple.
Back cover photograph, Jacqueline Pemberton

ISBN: 9 781999848958

Printed by Printdomain Ltd,

The right of Jacqueline Woods to be identified as the
author of this work has been asserted by her in
accordance with Section 77 of the Copyright, Designs
and Patents Act 1988.

This book is copyright. Subject to statutory exception
and to provisions of relevant collective licensing
agreements, no reproduction of any part may take
place without the written consent of the author.

Acknowledgements

'An Aldeburgh Sky' published in 'Heritage' Blue Door Press in collaboration with Aldeburgh Poetry 2017

'Remember Me' published by Milestones 'The Poetry Anthology WOL 2017' www.writeoutloud.net

'Please Hear What I'm not Saying' 2018 – Isabelle Kenyon's MIND anthology.flyonthewallpoetry.co.uk

'I have Learnt' published in WOLF anthology (Wolverhampton Library Festival 2018.)

"When the stars threw down their spears" published in Translating Chronic Pain - Lancaster University.

My thanks to Rita and Paul of Preeta Press for all their patience and for making this book possible.

Front Cover 'In the Shade' and illustrations by Julia Temple.

Julia is a very talented artist living in Suffolk and is also a dear friend whom I have known for over fifty years.
She helped me to solve my Maths problems when we were 12 and has helped me with many other problems throughout our adult lives. She has always been there for me with her calm, attentive and generous nature and I owe her a great debt of gratitude.
She first illustrated my poems in 1969 in the school magazine and I am honoured that she agreed to illustrate some of the poems in this, my new collection.
Thanks Julia!

Contents

I Have Learnt

To spell my name correctly.
Tie my laces; unpick labels.

I have learnt not to visit the past too often.
But leave her to doze in the mid-day sun.

I have learnt not to be afraid of getting lost
That sometimes it's better without a map.

I have faced my own mortality
And learnt to dance, despite the dark.

I have grown with my children,
Learnt wisdom through their eyes.

I have learnt that flesh is warmer than armour,
And holding is worth hurting.

And I will learn to say hello
Without dreading the next goodbye.

And learnt to leave the table
When love has long departed.

Eventually I will learn the difference
Between baring my soul and unpeeling my skin.

Catch a Falling Star

I am collecting memories like lucky pebbles in the pocket of a
winter coat.
Moments honeyed; warm as whispers.
A secret treasure chest amidst the debris.
I want to bring them back.
To hold them in cupped hands,
Breathe new life on them,
Feel them glow, revive and live again in heart and mind.
See again for the first time the night view across Victoria Harbour,
Listen to the symphony of the Super Trees in Singapore Bay,
Watch the sunset on Aldeburgh beach,
Swim with my dad in Suffolk tides.
I want to be waiting for Leonard to skip on stage to caress me
with his words.
I want to pose again for that photo with my children by my side,
Smiling in the sunshine.
I want to hug my poetry for the first and best time,
I want to turn the corner in the hospital to
 see my daughter with her baby:
Shock of golden hair, warble of new-born
cry, first touch of milky skin.
I want to bathe after my operation, soapy
water healing the hurt.
I want to hear the call of his love echoing
through lost years.
I want to be 12 years old and dancing to
Perry Como,
Believing that I could:
 'Catch a falling star
 Put it in my pocket
 And never let it fade away'.

2

An Aldeburgh Sky

The sun is setting on this festival
As I walk narrow streets back to my car,
Bracing myself against Suffolk winds,
Stooped and hooded,
Heavy with words.
And in the seagulls' cries
I hear the call of the herring girls
At the end of their day.
Pink hands raw with work,
Slicing, gutting slippery fish,
Flung into bottomless barrels.

In my souvenir bag I carry poetry,
Words fathomed from turbulent seas,
Hours sifting through sand
To find a pearl of light,
Shared today amongst this gathering
Of poets: hungry for language,
Born of this landscape:
Its desolate glory.
And as I travel home to warm memories
I hear the echo of the tired girls
Beneath a silver herring sky.

The Three of Us

Friends walking the same country path
We often walked when we were young,
Life and school holidays
Hovered before us.

You with your sketch pad,
Pencil propped behind your ear,
Me with my notebook
Of anxious verse.

We would find a spot to settle down
Near the river Orwell with its bow bridge
Reaching across a sky
Hungry for land.

Sometimes you would sketch me,
Pink flares and cotton smock,
A slide in my hair,
A faraway look in my eyes.

It's over forty years since I went away
Always hoping to return as more than a visitor
From a northern town that never quite
Became my home.

You stayed in Suffolk, stayed married
And lived a cloistered life
In the pink country cottage
Of my dreams.

My walls are full of your paintings,
My drawer stacked with letters
Spanning the years of our
Separated lives.

We pause awhile to admire the view,
Unable to walk as fast these days.
Our younger selves would think us very old
And long past dreaming.

Manea Station

The train stops at Manea: the station before Ely.
No one gets off or on but there is a woman waiting at the crossing,
A dark haired beauty out for a walk on a Sunday evening.
She is smiling to herself and I resist the urge to wave.
I want to be her; young and confident, decisions yet unmade
and so much more of life ahead of me.

This land is flat. Not the flat of a slap
but a languorous body relaxing on a sofa
or floating on a sea washed sky.
Pink cottages, brown farms, punctuate the earth,
Lights flicker from doll's house windows,
sheltering generations.

This used to be my home before he took me north
where I lost more than my Suffolk accent.
I return even though there are no arms
left to greet me: no one waiting at the station.
Light fades and the sky blushes into sleep.
I hold its hand but gradually the land slips from my grasp
until all I see is my own reflection and the misty image
of my fellow travellers as we journey on to our final destination.

Falling

'You've dropped your equilibrium',
Aunt Maud used to say
And every time I would look down.

Dad said I didn't have the balance to ride a bike,
And my school was just up the road
Anyway.

Mum made me terrified of falling pregnant,
I never let a boy do much more than
Kiss me.

Someone fell in love with me once
And I married him,
Not thinking.

Then I fell for someone else's lies
Whose eyes held promises he
Could not keep.

I stopped eating for a while
And the weight fell off me like
A coat.

Now I am old I wear an alarm
Round my neck,

Just in case I fall.

Math's lesson

'Stand up class and sit down when you know the answer.'
Mr Davis, did you know how much I prayed
you wouldn't pick on me?
And you never did, apart from that one time
when my friend was not there to help.

You pointed and I stuttered a response,
 'Stand up girl!'
My double sin: to be both dumb and deceitful.
My skirt stuck to the back of my legs,
Someone giggled behind me.

I stared at the circuitry of scrawls and symbols
knowing there would be no light bulb moment,
No revelation however much you probed
 my muddy brain
I would never find the Damascus road.

I had watched you interrogate other
pupils until they trembled
and couldn't speak,
But this time it was my stupidity exposed,
My ignorance lay bare.

You walked towards me,
pebble eyes peered
through bottle glasses,
Brylcreem slick hair,
A squeezed spot on your chin.

'Look at the board girl!'
My eyes watered as the numbers blurred,
You waited, then strode back to add another clue,
White string vest tight beneath
your nylon shirt.

My foolishness perplexed you,
Fear prickled my skin as
I prepared for humiliation.
You nipped a stub of chalk and slowly
drew a dunce's cap in the corner of the board.

Eventually someone whispered
the answer,
You led the mock applause,
I didn't cry till later.

Reading Aloud

Every night before I said my prayers
My mother read from story books,
Her honeyed curls poking
above the parapet of pages.

My favourite was the 'Wishing Chair'
which sprouted wings and transported
Peter, Molly and a Pixie
to different worlds and wonderful adventures.

I bought my rocking chair
three months before I married
from a Habitat Store which was closing down.
It travelled with us each time we moved,

But even with cushions it was never comfortable.
I liked the look of it: the crisscross webbing of the seat,
rockers smooth as treble clefs,
the dark stains where the joints were singed together.

Eventually I consigned it to the garden shed
where the sun bleached the wood
and the webbing began to fray.

I know that if I had a child's imagination
my chair would come to life one night,
sprout wings and take me to
different worlds and wonderful adventures.

De-clutter

Drawers deep with yellowed lesson plans and essays,
Bin bags pregnant with papers
I should have thrown out years ago.
Get Well cards from people once in my life,
A dried rose from a bouquet.

Then my wedding photograph emerges,
The one they printed in the Evening Star.

Recycle!
Let it become confetti,
Re-form to a white sheet,
A blank canvas to start again.

I hold it one last time.

Thirty years have gone and it's a cliché but we look so young,
I had wanted a Laura Ashley dress with fresh flowers in my hair
But mum said the nylon one from BHS looked better.
He is in a dark blue suit, wide tie and trousers.
His hair is longer, curlier.

My hand rests on his shoulder; his arm encircles my waist,
Blue bridesmaids stand like skittles behind us.
The guests are bundled in a corner.

We fix our smiles for the camera,
Our eyes half closed
Against a sharpened sun.

Leaving the Table

Today you texted me condolences
Using his first name
As if he was your friend.
You had heard it on the news,
'Trump victorious', 'Leonard Cohen: dead.'

You used to call him 'Len Nerd',
Music to slit your wrists to,
Master of the miserable,
King of the shabby bedsit.

Three years ago, that night
In my apartment
You had insisted
I play his latest album,
'I want to give Len Nerd a chance,' you said.

Even before the first track had finished
I felt your boredom sucking the air,
 I let you kiss my mouth to 'Marianne,'
Stroke my thighs to 'Field Commander Cohen,'
Play with my breasts to 'Gypsy Wife,'
Nibble my neck to 'Bird on a Wire.'

But your moan in my ear to 'Hallelujah'
Was more than I could bear,
And gathering my soul together
I pressed eject
On you, forever.

Brief Encounter

He got on the train carrying flowers.
 I was slumped in the corner,
Grey with disappointment,

'They're for my girlfriend; we had a row.'
'They're beautiful; 'good idea',
And I smiled as if part of a conspiracy.

We chatted and our words are lost now
And the journey from Manchester
Has blurred with the other
Thousand journeys I have taken,

But as I stood to leave the train
He pulled two flowers from the bouquet,
He had to tug to get them out.

'For you,' he said
And offered me the pink carnations.

I brushed the flowers against my lips
And as the train pulled off
I wanted to turn and wave,

But never did.

"When the stars threw down their spears"

I have William Blake and a glass of water
on my bedside table.
My lamp is touch sensitive, dimming gradually
beneath the pulse of my fingertips,
My curtains are thick velvet with tiny sequin stars

I try to follow a routine, keeping myself awake
until my eyelids ache.
I try to befriend the night, wary
that her cloak conceals a blade
to pierce the heart when least expected.
I have felt the soft flesh of sleep
turn to sandpaper, rasping me back
to the underbelly of unanswered questions
and the prickled blood of unwashed guilt.

The television I bought five years ago
sits in the corner of my room.
It helped me through those morphine nights
where my lung-drain, like a sick umbilical cord
snagged from my side.
I would watch Countdown at 3 a.m., clasping
the puppetry of sign language like a charm.

Tomorrow my new feather duvet should arrive,
It is soft and pink, like the inside of a womb.

Womb

My mouth mimics its shape.
A secret place.
A cup, a cradle,
Moist and warm.

It grew inside me
Like an orchid, opening,
Pink and pulsing
It bled for me.

Held within its lining
The first nugget of being,
Nurtured a legacy of love,
Kept my babies safe
As they blossomed
Then burst to life.

The core of my womanhood,
We grew together.
Years of ripening
Followed by a timely slumbering,
We should have ended our days
Together.

But now my womb is sick,
Rebellious cells
Threaten my existence.
It feels like a betrayal.

Why do I mourn its leaving?
And on our last night together
Press my hands across
My soft white belly
And feel the shudder of ghosts
Departing?

The Unfolding

Clean as a scalpel
It rests on my door mat.
I hold this moment.
Linger in the fragile joy
Of unread seconds,
Take comfort in the half light
Of undrawn curtains.

I will plan my journey, slowly.
Think how I will uncurl
And unfold my body,
Gently unhinge my joints,
Get my balance.
Then push down on my feet
Letting my ankles take the strain
As I rise and open my eyes,
Stand up straight.

Next, count the distance,
The breaths I must take.
Feign a lightness of step,
Feel the cool slide of vinyl
Beneath my bare soles,
Try to focus as I bend
And scoop the letter up.

Try not to shake
As I open the envelope,
Unfold the page, see my name.
There's no need to read it all at once,
Just take a few words at a time,
Select and quantify; make things easy.
There *will* be relief in knowing.

This is the hardest part,
The worst of times.
In a moment I will move... walk... read... know.
But for now,
There is no rush.

Chorley Train Station

An Asylum of white tiles and metal benches.
I want to clothe this room with poetry,
Soften the seats with cushions,
Hide the naked window behind silken drapes.
I have shivered many hours within these walls,
Watching the screen for delays and cancellations:
Lost trains, lost drivers, caught in a no man's land between
Preston and the Universe.
Found temporary fellowship with kindred travellers,
All needing to be somewhere else than Chorley,

Today, this soulless room shudders through me even more.
I apologise to my son for the sparseness of this place,
The trains always running late,
But the delay gives us a few more moments before he leaves,
Begins a journey he will not complete until tomorrow night,
A continent and climate far away.
This is the bleakest time when the months stretch out
In gnawing hunger: starving me of his presence.
The train arrives and I cling to the damp smell of his duffel coat,
His shy smile. Watch, as he struggles with his case and finds a seat,
Wave, as he slips from my life again.

A Mindful Reunion

We meet in silence
Clutching blankets brought from home,
Holding memories from a year ago
When scars were raw,
Heads disguised by wigs
And tears too salt to weep.

I found words difficult then.
'Body scan'
Was not a mindful exercise
But a machine at the end of a corridor.
There were places in my body
I could not touch with thought.

Like chrysalis we scatter the floor
Each section of our being
Revisited with childlike curiosity,
Sensations magnified,
The tickle of wool, the press of cotton.
A forgotten ache from an ankle.

Our teacher's voice
Both lesson and lullaby
Returning to the breath
Again and again
We try to train our thoughts;
Naughty as puppies
With Baskerville bites

I find peacefulness within the ordinary,
Rest my head in the soft cushion of a second
Savouring the beauty of this moment both
Rooted in earth and reaching for stars.

Remembrance Day.

The Acer is alive with sunlight,
Enriching this dull November day,
Burnished with a treasure of branches,
A gloss of leaves freshly washed by rain.

I stand in the synonym of silence,
A brief reverence for the years
I never noticed its growing,
How it changed, as my life changed.

The gardener wants to trim it,
To tame a few unruly branches,
Make it symmetrical and ensure
It doesn't take over the garden.

Once, Mum had my hair cut short
To make it grow stronger,
My curls littered our kitchen floor,
Sad as unrequited kisses.

The leaves are pinpricked
With gemstones of light,
Their tips thinning like the grandeur
Of a ball gown tired from dancing.

Soon the bare days will come,
Leaves will drench the patio
While the tree shivers unheeded,
And I try hard not to remember.

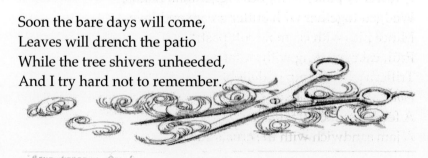

'Remembrance Day'

Dad's Heart

The hospital rang at 2am,
Mum was making her way downstairs,
Wearing her pink fluffy dressing gown and slippers,
Vulnerable as a little girl.
I made tea and started a list
To fill the gaps till morning,
Needing to share the burden of a grief
We had not yet begun to lift.
They said he was smiling as they helped him into bed.
Made a joke with the nurses: poorly as he was.
I had never wanted to believe
My dad's heart would stop beating,
That there would be a time when he was no longer
At the station to meet me, take my suitcase,
Ask me what kind of journey I'd had,
Tell me where he'd parked the car.
I wish he hadn't always passed the phone to mum
So quickly, stayed a while and had a chat,
And I wish that you had known him and the warmth of his smile
And I could find the words in this poem, fitting to his memory.

Mum's afternoon tea

Then:
A tower of pink meringues bigger than hands,
Wedged together with butter cream and love.
Mince pies with crumble soft pastry,
Fruit cake bursting with sultanas,
Trifle: a jelly swamp of delight.
Now:
A feeder beaker of weak tea,
A jam sandwich with the crusts cut off.

Remember Me

'Do I know you dear?'
The question she asks
me every morning
with her lemon smile
and tepid eyes.

'I'm Denise, your daughter,'
I say to the empty space
between us.

I wish she'd had a sudden death and
not this sleeping sickness
that makes a drought
 of memory.

I show her photographs:
My first birthday,
First day at school,
Graduation,
The wedding.

I want to plant a seed
within her frozen womb,
Let her recall that first flicker,
How she touched her belly
with a secret smile.

Remember the pain of labour
as she struggled to give birth,
Held me against her swollen breast
with joy.

Let her start again
from *my* first breath,
Return to find the child in *me*,
The awkward adolescent,
The middle-aged woman
Who longs to be hugged.
Start the journey of *our* past
again.

'Are you sure dear?
I thought I had a son.'

Surfaces

My skin has simmered for too long,
Dried to a wrinkled toughness
That catches the throat.
I am divorcing my skeleton,
Flesh separating from bones
it once cleaved to like
a climber on a rock face:
taut and agile.

Now, it dangles pathetically,
Hoping to be rescued with
a potion, Botox or a
surfeit of spa weekends,
But it has sagged
beyond redemption.

Underarms, inner thighs, pucker in petulance,
I pinch my skin and it no longer protests but
crumples: an obscene scrotum of creases.
Magnified, my cheeks are a fossilised
landscape of spider veins and calcified craters,
Scarred by the elements,
Battered by the years.

My features are folding,
Surrendering to gravity,
Sinking into dullness.
I avoid changing rooms,
Prefer to undress alone
in half-light; teased only
by the flickering moth
of memory.

The Brittle Thread

'Are you pregnant?'
She thinks my daughter is me
forty five years ago.

Her acid words seep through
generations,
Like an old photograph, disintegrating.
Faceless boyfriends she always
disapproved of; certain
they were only after, *one thing.*

Demanding that I *save myself for marriage,*
as she had done,
The virginal white of my wedding dress
chafing my untouched body.

I see again the back street I would
have been thrown into,
The gutter I would drink from,
The swelling of my bastard belly.

Would my dad have rescued me
in his Ford Cortina?
Forged through the impenetrable fog
of her misguided morals to shine
a beam of love for me to hold.

Or would they both have left me
in the squalid darkness,
Trying to sever the umbilical cord
with blunt and rusted scissors?

A Befriender:

I meet them in their sitting down years,
Moulded into high winged armchairs,
Forgotten mugs of tea
Rest on cream coloured trollies.

Meals and medication
Consume their lives,
Pendants flop on food
stained jumpers.

Sideboards are a swathe of smiling faces
They rarely see.
China cabinets stacked with tea sets
Too posh to use or part with.

Their bathrooms have grab rails,
Raised seats, non-slip mats
And in the corner
A stack of pads.

But when they talk
Their lives light up.

Ida danced on a moonlit beach
With a handsome man from Italy
She wore a red rose
In her long auburn hair.

Vinnie was a biker,
Fought the Mods at Brighton,
He could strip a bike and a woman
In the blink of an eye.

Maureen led a busy life,
Head of the typing pool at the Coop,
She kept the girls in order
And flirted with the boss.

They talk of times
When legs could race,
Hands could grasp
And flesh was bold.

The dreams they had,
The loves they lost,
The holidays they went on,
The trip they nearly took.

I fill in my next visit
On their empty calendar.

Outside, the air is fresher
And my future nearer
Than I realise.

Colour me Beautiful

Wash me of boring beige, limp lilac, morose magnolia.
Paint me again.
My hair India Yellow, smelling of spice and sunshine.
Let me have Lulworth Blue eyes for lovers to drown,
Transform my Off White skin to Slipper Satin,
Stroke my cheeks with Cinder Rose,
Splash my teeth with Brilliant White,
Lips Incarnadine; irresistible,
My voice bursting with Pink Geranium.
Thighs taste of Dorset Cream on Sunday afternoon,
And Red Earth on Sunday night.
Mahogany arms encircle you,
Blazer Red nails grip you
And Indigo Dream flood
Your Dead Salmon world
With Rainbows.

Annabelle means Joy

Reluctant first to enter this world,
Now you consume it with your eyes,
Bluer than summer holidays,
Deeper than wishing wells,
Wide as happiness.

Too busy for sleep
You drink in new sensations,
Marvel at the world
Just beyond your grasp.
Captivate with your wobbly
Smile and dancing hands.

White noise and warm milk
Coax you for a while
But the chime of your name
Wakes you to curiosity again.

Bright futures stretch before you
Annabelle,
May you always travel well.

Bath Time

I send you this little plastic duck wrapped
in the uncountable layers of my love,
Imagine your giggles brighter than bubbles
as you play with her at bath time.
I sing to you across our distant lives
for all the bath times I will miss
and the ones I will enjoy.

To my great, great, great granddaughter

I bequeath my diaries.
You will have kind eyes
And a warm heart.
Understand my good intentions,
Realise that no pain was deliberately inflicted,
No hurt contrived and that these pages show
A woman struggling to be free.
My faded photograph sits on your mantelpiece,
Reveals a family likeness,
The way we smile, the dimple on our chin
But cannot catch the sepia soul within.

My voice speaks to you through generations,
Be gentle; you have the cushion of history.
Mountains which seemed insurmountable
Have long been climbed and conquered,
Scars which roared through endless nights
Softened to a whimper.
Lost lovers no longer need to be found.
What once consumed has been consumed.
The grand becomes the trivial and despair
At last finds consolation.

As you read I will reach to hold your hand,
Feel my dry flesh breathe and pulse again.
You can heal the hurt of those who read
My words in secret,
And make amends for what was left unsaid.
Time folds her aching wings
Within these pages,
Let my restless spirit sleep
Beneath your kindly gaze.